Saved from the Stones

Vanessa Bermudez

Dedication

I dedicate this book to each of my children:
Steven, Omar, Kristian, Johana and Shaila,
who always loved me despite all the suffering
in the midst of the storm.

To my beloved husband,
a courageous and mighty man of God.
Thank you for loving me and giving me the forgiveness
that I so desperately needed.
Thank you for loving Jesus more than you love
yourself.

To my beloved Savior,
the one who extended His loving and forgiving arms
one day and said to me,
***Woman, where are the ones
that were condemning you?
Go and sin no more.***

Acknowledgements

To my daughter Shaila, the one I always knew would help write my book.

To Pastor Noel Alarcon, his wife Lorena, and all the brothers and sisters of Fort Cayton Asamblea de Dios, for their constant love and encouragement to continue in the faith when it was most difficult. The acceptance and grace you showed to my husband and me at our darkest hour were a beautiful, tangible example of the love that Christ has for us. You loved us and pointed us not to our wrong, not to you, and not to your church, but to Christ, and for that we will forever be grateful. With a full heart, Juan still tells of the "small church" that loved him. Thank you!

I could not allow myself to go any further without thanking my husband once more. Always selfless, you encouraged me to move forward with this project and gave me your full support, without which I could not have done this. I truly have seen the Lord grow His love and forgiveness in you: such a beautiful thing to witness. Thank you!

Table of Contents

Introduction

My heart's desire in writing this book is to impart faith and peace to women who have been impacted in some way by the sin of adultery. There may be some women in need of repentance. I want you to know that it is available to you; and, for the heart that has repented, there is peace in the midst of and after the storm.

Through the years, I have noticed the unpopularity of the topic of adultery, not only in the world – and understandably so, because of the immorality it concerns – but also in the church and among believers. I have felt the painful sting of rejection and loneliness from both sides. This has brought me to believe that the avoidance of this topic stems from the shame that such sin bears. The discomfort that I have witnessed surrounding the topic of adultery has, in the past, left me taken aback and often feeling isolated in what once was my battle. I was never prepared to face the realization that the battle would not be in my "one failure", but that it would follow me for the greater extent of my walk with Christ. It was heart-wrenching to see those around me living out the roles of the religious leaders and Pharisees in the text of **John 8:2-11 (NLT):**

. . . but early the next morning he was back again at the Temple. A crowd soon gathered, and he sat down and taught them. As he was speaking, the teachers of religious law and the Pharisees brought a woman who had been caught in the act of adultery. They put her in front of the crowd.

"Teacher," they said to Jesus, "this woman was caught in the act of adultery. The Law of Moses says to stone her. What do you say?"

They were trying to trap him into saying something they could use against him, but Jesus stooped down and wrote in the dust with his finger. They kept demanding an answer, so he stood up again and said, "All right, but let the one who has never sinned throw the first stone!" Then he stooped down again and wrote in the dust.

When the accusers heard this, they slipped away one by one, beginning with the oldest, until only Jesus was left in the middle of the crowd with the woman. Then Jesus stood up again and said to the woman, "Where are your accusers? Didn't even one of them condemn you?"

"No, Lord," she said.

And Jesus said, "Neither do I. Go and sin no more."

In both the church and the world, people who learned of my sin quickly picked up "stones" and were ready to hurl them at me. In fact, some did, with their words or painful actions. But, to my relief, the grace experienced by the adulterous woman in this passage was also extended to me by God. He longs to give that same grace to you as well.

I encourage you to abandon yourself totally to His loving arms so that, when the accompanying judgment from others occurs – not only in the world, but also with some believers in the church – you will be standing firm in His love and forgiveness. HE HAS YOU!

CHAPTER I
He Cares for You

The burden that I carry and have carried for years – the burden that has led me to write this book – is truly one given to me by the Lord. My burden has been for women who have suffered the devastating pain of an adulterous relationship, have repented, and are seeking redemption. Our God is an amazing God and desires freedom for us all: I know this because He spoke to me. By speaking to me about this very sin, He birthed in me the desire to reach out to other women who have experienced a similar situation.

Allow me to explain further. One Sunday, while sitting in church and waiting for the service to begin, I heard the Lord say to me, *Vanessa, look back*. Now, I typically sit within the first ten rows of a church that seats around one thousand. I quickly turned back and surveyed the congregation. He then proceeded to ask,

What do you see? I responded within myself, not really sure where this was going, *Well, I see a room full of people, Lord.* To that, He answered, **Consider the fact that among these people is the sin of adultery.**

In the moment, these words didn't carry too much value. I was surprised by the insight and a bit perplexed as to its purpose and timing, but I went on without considering in depth the words spoken to me by Him. It wasn't until later, when the Lord reminded me of these very words and inspired the idea of a book centered around them, that their weight and value actually sank into my heart. He showed me that He sees and cares for women who are suffering as a result of this sin. I know His heart's desire is to bring healing into the suffering. After all, He did it for me, and I asked myself, *Why not for others?* He inspired me to reach out to women who have fallen into adultery – to reach out to your hearts and assure you that in Christ there is peace, there is redemption, there is freedom. In His redemptive sacrifice, your spouse and your family can find faith to overcome; but, let me assure you that this victory is found in Christ alone.

Scripture to hold on to:

Peace I leave with you; my peace I give to you. Not as the world gives do I give to you. Let not your hearts be troubled, neither let them be afraid.

John 14:27 (ESV)

I have said these things to you, that in me you may have peace. In the world you will have tribulation. But take heart; I have overcome the world.

John 16:33 (ESV)

No, in all these things we are more than conquerors through him who loved us.

Romans 8:37 (ESV)

CHAPTER II
The Beginning of My Journey

Our story begins in the year 1969. My husband and I were young and completely unaware of what we were walking into when we decided to marry one another. My husband was 18 at that time, and I was only 14. You may be wondering how it was possible for two people to marry so young; well, at that age, as you may have experienced – either personally or through children of your own – Juan and I thought we knew it all. We told ourselves that we loved each other and that that was enough. So, without any parental consent, we eloped. Once our parents realized what we had done, they had no choice but to allow what had already been decided by Juan and me. Both sets of parents signed agreements after the fact, permitting and acknowledging our marriage, which was then made official by a magistrate.

I would like to take a moment before continuing with the story to emphasize the importance of pre-marital counseling. Marriage is a great responsibility, shared equally by both people involved. Marriage is nothing to be taken lightly. It is a commitment. It is a covenant.

We were married on July 1st. As you can imagine, we began this journey without any idea of what it meant. My husband was young and came from a home in which a healthy model of marriage was not taught. In reality, I was the only one who took our covenant of marriage seriously. He lived as though he had no commitment to me. There was a lot of partying, alcohol, and infidelity on his part. This happened constantly. I stayed only because of the deep love and loyalty I had for him. Even when he behaved so recklessly, I could still see the good in him. He was not a bad man. He was just executing learned behavior that he had witnessed while growing up.

Years passed, and I found myself still in the same place in marriage, covenanted with a man who lived only to satisfy himself. As you can imagine, if one is not cautious, one can become bitter. I still loved him, but the hurt and anger began to build up inside me. I cannot fully express the importance of guarding your heart. You see, I did not know then what this meant. I was not a born-again Christian, so I was not familiar with this powerful concept from the Word of God.

Perhaps some of you reading these lines are not yet born again, or have not received Jesus as the Lord and Savior of your life. If you have, then you know what I am talking about. Many in this world can and will hurt you, but how that hurt affects you depends on what you decide to do with it. It depends on the condition of your heart. Just as it states in **Proverbs 4:23 (NLT): "Guard your heart above all else, for it determines the course of your life."** I caution you now because I didn't know better then; and, unfortunately, I chose the hard-hearted, bitter road.

Fifteen years and three babies later, my heart was heavy and full of turmoil. All this time, I was still loving and forgiving my husband – but with my own might, and not with that of a personal Savior. I was growing more and more bitter without even realizing it. Finally, a day came when bitterness and sorrow took total control of my life. That was when I encountered myself face-to-face with deep depression, a devastating disease that encloses you in deep sorrow; but, I will talk more of this phase of my life in the following chapter. For now, I will focus on what this bitterness did to my relationship with my husband.

I vividly remember judging him harshly for all the times he was unfaithful to me and telling my family and friends how angry I was at him for doing what he had done. His unfaithfulness and my bitterness came together to cause a divide so great that, for a moment, it felt that we were no longer one – if we ever had been. In that moment, I deliberately closed the door of my heart to my husband.

Once I had made this decision, every "wifely privilege" thereafter became robotic: a duty with no heart behind it. I was emotionally drained, with nothing to give to my husband. Every beautiful castle I had built in the sky literally lay in shambles before me. Perhaps, if I had shared what I was going through, someone could have helped me, but I didn't – not even with family and friends. I buried everything further down, and the bitterness continued to grow.

CHAPTER III
The Fall

In 1981, due to my husband's military service, we were stationed in Panama for 3 years. Our command sponsor, who was assigned to help military families, made sure we had a smooth transition into the new base. He was a Christian man. He and his wife immediately "witnessed" to our family – meaning, they talked to us about the Gospel of Jesus Christ. Unfortunately, their efforts were not received by us; but, even so, they never stopped loving us and extending to us their kindness.

After some time, we settled in and made a new circle of friends. We began to entertain ourselves with parties in which these friends always accompanied us. There were times when I thought to myself, *Maybe this can help with my darkening and hardening heart. Maybe I could be happy again.* And, for a while, it worked. Going out and partying with friends made me feel happy. I became reacquainted with what it felt like to have fun and be carefree; but, these feelings only ever lasted for a moment. Misery and loneliness waited patiently until the temporary stimulation of "fun" had left, reminding me that they were still there and still in control of my mind.

About 8 months after arriving in Panama, I invested in a friendship that would alter the trajectory of my life. This male friend began, in the most innocent of ways, to fill the spaces that were left empty by my husband and the circumstances of my life.

Allow me to pause here and advise you not to engage in friendship with a member of the opposite sex by sharing your deep emotions and struggles. You will open the door for an intimacy that should only be practiced with your spouse.

Our friendship twisted one day when we found ourselves alone. In that moment, what I so harshly judged my husband for – what I hated most in him – the hideous sin of adultery, I fell into myself. After all was said and done, I immediately felt vile. All the morals and high standards that I had always measured myself with no longer meant anything. A wave of guilt came over me and I felt, even more than usual, a deep, deep sorrow. Never had I imagined that I could feel worse than in years past; but there, in that moment, I did.

Not long after, I suffered a nervous breakdown. I could no longer handle the pressure of what I had done, and I fell into a deep depression. It felt like I had fallen into a deep pit, one of hopelessness, where no one could reach me. My husband, without knowledge of what had occurred, helped during my breakdown in the best way he knew how: calling for medical assistance. Nothing seemed to work. After receiving psychiatric and psychological help – even seeing my therapist every week for a year and taking four different drugs daily – I still experienced only minimal relief. I remained in deep depression. I spent most of my days in bed, unable to connect with myself, my family, or the world.

CHAPTER IV
Redemption for Once and for All

By this time, I had developed a good relationship with the wife of my husband's command sponsor. I confessed to her what I had done and shared all that I was going through. She didn't look down on me; instead, she took good care of me. As kind a woman as she was, she even sent her housekeeper to help with the chores and children while I faced my dreary circumstances. I was so grateful for my friend and her willingness to help. I was also grateful for Ramona, the housekeeper – who, it turns out, would not only assist me in the care of my home and children, but in the healing of my own heart.

Ramona was kind, quiet in spirit and yet a very strong woman of faith. On her first day of coming to assist at my house she presented the Gospel to me. She found me lying in bed, as was common at this time of my life, and she said,

"Ms. Vanessa, I know you are in a place that I couldn't even begin to imagine, because you are the one living it, but I will tell you one thing: if you let the Lord come into your life, I am not promising that everything will be solved immediately, but I will say that He will help you carry the weight of what you are going through."

At that moment, I thought to myself, *I've tried everything else – therapy, medicine, my own remedies – and nothing has helped. What do I have to lose in trying this as well?*

I asked her, "What do I need to do?"

She replied, "You just say a simple prayer, asking the Lord to forgive you for all your sins, and invite him into your life."

When I acknowledged her words and she helped me say the prayer, I didn't quite feel anything; but, I do know now that at that very moment, God deposited in me enough faith to believe that change for my life and my family was possible through Christ. As Jesus said in the **Gospel of Matthew 19:26 (ESV): "But Jesus looked at them and said, 'With man this is impossible, but with God all things are possible.'"**

A week passed, and I received a call from my friend inviting me to a women's Bible study. I decided to attend. When the Bible study was over, there was a moment of prayer. We all stood in a circle holding hands, and the leader of the Bible study asked for any prayer requests. With a heavy heart and a tinge of desperation, I asked for prayer for my husband, our children, and me.

The following week came, and it was time for my weekly therapy session. I went to my psychologist's office, and the secretary gave me the "ok" to go inside. I opened the door and greeted him. To my surprise, he brought to my attention something I had not realized I wasn't doing anymore. He said,

"Vanessa, you are smiling."

For the first time, I realized that my smile had been wiped off my face for months. My reply to him was that I had been experiencing a joy I had never felt before. I think that was my first time telling someone that I had received the Lord Jesus as my forgiving Savior. It was my first witness! That day, I decided to put to an end to my therapy sessions.

I soon became a member of this small church that my friend was part of. The pastor and his wife, Noel and Lorena Alarcon, embraced me with loving arms, as did the congregation. They completely disregarded my past and what I had done, and they gave me the emotional help I needed at that time. Not once did I feel judged by any of them, and yet they all knew my situation. A sense of freedom overwhelmed me. It was a wonderful feeling to be accepted and loved despite their knowledge of my wrongdoing. I will never forget these brothers and sisters in Christ. They extended such grace and helped me carry the weight of my burden with support and encouragement. They cried and prayed with me in the midst of my pain.

That, to me, was my second encounter with grace, the first being what the Lord extended to me upon my conversion. He has so freely given us this wonderful grace. ***Grace means that God has given us free and unmerited favor through Jesus Christ for the forgiving of our sins.*** So, if we have freely received this grace, then we should be ready to give it with the same measure. As **Matthew 10:8b (NIV)** states: **"'Freely you have received, freely give.'"**

This is what that church family did for me.

CHAPTER V
My Story Turns Dark

The more I read the Bible, prayed, and fasted, the more I was convicted of the fact that I was living a lie. Every time I looked at my husband, I became more certain that I needed to confess my sin to him. Finally, after much prayer and fasting, I decided to do so. I spoke with my pastor and his wife about my intentions and sought advice. My pastor, agreeing that it was the right thing to do, tried to prepare me for the possible outcomes of my confession. He made me aware of the fact that I could lose my husband. At that moment, I felt the sting of fear, but God deposited in my heart the faith to believe that He would carry me, and faith overcame.

The pastor, his wife, and I arranged to meet at my house on a Saturday. I told my husband they were coming and asked if he could stay home until their visit was over. He agreed. Waiting on the day of that meeting, my mind sometimes wandered into the moment in which I was to confess. What frightened me the most was the thought of his reaction: what would he say? What might he do? When haunted by these anxious questions, I prayed, and again felt peace.

I still remember everything so vividly. The meeting was set for 2 o'clock that Saturday afternoon. The time came, and we all gathered in the living room. We made small talk for a few minutes. At last, the moment arrived when my pastor turned to my husband. He told him I had something to share – something that I wanted him to know.

He then turned to me and said, "This is the moment". Immediately, my body felt cold and weak, but I knew what I needed to do. It gave me great comfort that my pastor and his wife turned to each other and began praying. This gave me strength to begin my confession. Supported by their love and prayer, I told my husband what I had done. I confessed to him I had committed adultery.

I remember so clearly his response to my confession. He reacted with such anger and discomposure, and understandably so. He seemed enraged and confused, almost as if he were deciding whether or not to inflict harm on me. I felt consumed with remorse, and I asked him to forgive me. I also felt his immense pain. My heart, which was already broken, broke once again when I saw the suffering I had caused him.

He left the house immediately after gathering his thoughts. My pastor and his wife prayed for me and the family, and then they also left. And there I was, thinking about what had just happened – afraid, crying, but hopeful. I also felt a sense of relief from telling the truth. It was as if a heavy load had been lifted off me.

My husband did not return to our home for a week. He decided he'd rather stay at the barracks, the place in which single soldiers live. I called the barracks so I could speak to him, but the sergeant in charge did not let me. When the kids asked for his whereabouts, the only thing I could tell them was, "He will be back." I was uncertain about his return, but I tried to hide this in an effort to make them feel better. That week, for me, was eternal. Fear tried to creep in, but the faith and peace I felt were stronger than any fear.

To my dismay, when my husband did return, he asked me to leave. He wanted me to take our middle child and the three-year-old. Even though the idea of leaving our oldest child behind broke my heart, I accepted it. Only God knew the feeling of desperation I was facing, so in those moments of distress, I sought Him wholeheartedly in prayer. Once again, he calmed my troubled heart. He spoke to me and assured me that He was going to bring me back home within two weeks.

His small, still voice gave comfort, peace, and faith to believe that He would carry out His promise.

Information really does get around quickly. Word of my failure spread like wildfire amongst our friends, and they began separating themselves from me. I remember a specific time when two friends of mine were talking at the entrance of a store. I approached them, and as I began to greet them, they looked at me with disdain and walked away without a word. My heart ached because of their slight, and for the first time, I realized how much judgment I would be forced to face. This was just the beginning of my walk with rejection.

It is so ironic to see the world judging you when it comes to adultery. In the world, women are harshly criticized for this action, whereas men often go unpunished. For years, I carried the shame of that day – along with the judgment of other people – on my shoulders. Yes, I was cleansed by the blood of the Lamb, but that was something only the Lord and my brothers and sisters in Christ could understand, not those of the world. It wasn't their fault. They were blinded to this truth. Only those who have been born again can understand the Kingdom of God and the working of His hand in our lives. Just as **John 3:3 (NLT)** states: **"Jesus replied, 'I tell you the truth, unless you are born again, you cannot see the Kingdom of God.'"** This reality was hard for me to face: I knew the great miracle He had done in me, but they – those of the world – did not.

I was brokenhearted from every angle: my own action, my husband's response, my upcoming departure, the separation of my family, and the loss of those who I thought were my friends. I didn't want to leave, but after seeking the Lord again in much prayer, God reminded me of the word He had given me. His promise – that I was going to return in two weeks – gave me the peace I needed to move forward in what was expected of me. I knew I would be home soon enough. I left with two of my boys and went to Georgia, U.S.A, to stay with my sister.

I am a firm believer that if you allow God to work in your life, He will bring about change, and every circumstance will serve a purpose. So, I continued my journey . . .

CHAPTER VI
My World Changes

While staying with my sister, I met a friend of hers who was a believer and follower of Christ. One night, this friend came to my sister's home for a visit and invited me to a prayer and fasting gathering. It was held in a small group that was part of the church she attended. Knowing how much I needed such an event, I accepted the invitation. I was so grateful I did! I was able to feel His peace, which reminded me of His Word in **Philippians 4:6-7 (ESV)**: **". . . do not be anxious about anything, but in everything by prayer and supplication with thanksgiving let your requests be made known to God. And the peace of God, which surpasses all understanding, will guard your hearts and your minds in Christ Jesus."**

The peace I experienced was truly beyond understanding. In a moment when most would think that suffering and sorrow were the only options, I asked for peace, and He gave it to me. All fear, dread, and worry were removed. But, I could only find this peace when I was abiding in Him. **"If you abide in me, and my words abide in you, ask whatever you wish, and it will be done for you." – John 15:7 (ESV)** Otherwise, I would feel the claws of fear trying to grab me and paralyze the faith and hope with which the Lord had reassured me.

After that wonderful experience was over, I visited the church – The House of the Father – the following Sunday with my sister's friend. I'm not quite sure why, but the name of this church really touched me. As I entered the worship center that Sunday, an overwhelming feeling of the Lord's presence came over me. I knew at that very moment He was in that place and had been always with me.

The service was about to end when the pastor gave a word of knowledge. The Holy Spirit had impressed upon him to tell the congregation that there was going to be healing for a person with cancer of the intestines. An elderly lady stood amidst the congregation and walked towards the pastor. He laid his hands on her and prayed, and she, by faith, received her healing. The Holy Spirit spoke to the pastor again, this time saying that there was going to be a baptism of the Holy Spirit. Being a Catholic in my earlier years, I did not know what the baptism of the Holy Spirit was; yet, still,

I heard in my spirit that the person he was referring to was me. I went to the front, and he laid hands on me and began to pray. In that moment, I received the baptism of the Holy Spirit and began speaking in other tongues. *(To know more about the baptism of the Holy Spirit, read Acts 2:1-13 and 10:44-46.)*

After this, an urge to study the Word and understand the baptism of the Holy Spirit took over me. In my study, I found that what had happened to me was scriptural and was also for a purpose: **"But you will receive power when the Holy Spirit comes on you; and you will be my witnesses in Jerusalem, and in all Judea and Samaria, and to the ends of the earth." – Acts 1:8 (NIV)**

The Lord began to manifest himself to me through visions, through the hearing of his audible voice, and through His Word. With each experience, the Lord reassured me that everything was going to work out for the good of my family. **Romans 8:28 (ESV) "And we know that for those who love God all things work together for good, for those who are called according to his purpose."** He really was invested in my life and cared about every detail of my family. And, just as I thought the Holy Spirit couldn't be more invested in me and in my family's ordeals, He brought to remembrance what He had spoken to me before I left Panama: that I would be home in two weeks.

I received a call from my husband almost two weeks into my time in Georgia. He told me I needed to come back home. He explained that our eldest son, who stayed with him in Panama when I left, had run away. He had called to inform my husband that he would not return home until I did. He was only 13 years old.

It is so sad to realize that your child's suffering is the outcome of your mistake. This was not the way nor the reason I wanted to be called back home, but God used this very moment to begin doing a much-needed work within our family, although it didn't seem like it at the time.

Upon my return to Panama and to our home, my husband made it very clear that he wanted nothing to do with me. He sat down with me and informed me, "You have come back to this home and to the kids, but you have not come home to me." At this very moment and with these very painful words, I realized why the Lord had baptized me with the Holy Spirit. I was going to need His power to be a witness to my husband, even in the most difficult times of the journey that lay ahead.

For three years, I experienced a trial that, without His power, I would not have been able to endure. During that time of my life, the Word of God was literally the bread of life to me. It was the only thing sustaining me spiritually, emotionally, and even mentally. **Matthew 4:4 (ESV)** says, **"But he answered,**

'It is written, "Man shall not live by bread alone, but by *every word* (emphasis mine) that comes from the mouth of God."'"'

Why? Because during that season, I went through a lot of emotional turmoil caused by my husband's behavior towards me. There were moments in which I lost respect and admiration for my husband. Still, the Holy Spirit kept reminding me that, if I wanted my husband to forgive me and trust me again, I needed to follow the Word and its instruction. I adapted the way Daniel prayed three times a day **(Daniel 6:10)**. I prayed morning, noon and evening, seeking God's strength and wisdom.

On a side note: when facing trials, dear friends, often times the last thing you want to do is seek God in prayer and maintain a spiritual discipline – this is if you have received the Lord as your personal Savior – but it is the thing you need most. The Word was my guidance for what to do next – and, more importantly, what not to do. Prayer was my only source of peace and fellowship with the One who, at the lowest point of my life, loved me unconditionally, understood me, and did not reject me.

What I desired most for my husband in the midst of our storm was for him to know my Savior. I wanted him to be able to experience what I had found: first, salvation, and then the peace that my Lord so freely and graciously gives. My journey with the Lord helped me to maintain faith that my husband could one day forgive me and believe in restoration for our marriage, just as I was believing. Yet, even in the midst of my faith, I still had to ask myself, *How am I going to do this when I am so torn inside by the past? When I sometimes feel so angry – and yet, still so eager to walk in my new life?*

CHAPTER VII
Inspiration to Become the Wife
I Needed to Be

While reading the Word one day, my eyes ran across a subtitle that immediately grabbed my interest: "Wives and Husbands". Naturally, my heart was hungry to hear anything that God had to say towards wives and husbands, considering the situation my husband and I were in. The passage was **I Peter 3:1-6 (ESV)**, which states:

> **Likewise, wives, be subject to your own husbands, so that even if some do not obey the word, they may be won without a word by the conduct of their wives, when they see your respectful and pure conduct. Do not let your**

adorning be external – the braiding of hair and the putting on of gold jewelry, or the clothing you wear – but let your adorning be the hidden person of the heart with the imperishable beauty of a gentle and quiet spirit, which in God's sight is very precious. For this is how the holy women *who hoped in God* (emphasis mine) **used to adorn themselves, by submitting to their own husbands, as Sarah obeyed Abraham, calling him lord. And you are her children, if you do good and do not fear anything that is frightening.**

Now, before I continue, I would just like to point out one thing. When this passage was written, I do not believe it was Peter's intent to say, "All women who trust in the Lord must now 'let themselves go' in the looks department. There shall be no more looking pretty." **No. Not so.** I believe it is important to care for our physical bodies. Look pretty. Feel lovely. Maintain a healthy lifestyle. Just do not place these things ahead of your inner self. See, Peter's intention was more to stress the importance of maintaining, just as one would for their home, the gardens and grounds of one's spirit. Peter was referring to the importance of upkeep in our spiritual lives in order to bear the fruit of "a gentle and quiet spirit", as well as to help us respect and honor our husbands. What shall we, as wives, gain for the Kingdom if we are beautiful on the outside yet wretched within ourselves, displaying anger, disrespect, and harshness towards our husbands? How, my dear friends, will that be a witness to them?

I digress. Returning to the story at hand: at that point in our marriage, when at moments I felt no respect and admiration for my husband, I needed to hear such an inspiration. Despite the Holy Spirit's ongoing work in me and my desire for reconciliation, my heart still wrestled at times, and even wanted to harden again. This passage gave me hope that I could change and be the woman God was calling me to be. I pleaded with the Lord to change my heart and soften it. I needed His help to become a woman and wife with a gentle and quiet spirit. I wanted nothing more than to display these attributes and for my husband's heart to be won over to Christ. I knew in the deepest part of my heart that, without the Lord's help and intervention, this change would not take place in my life.

Dying to self and your old ways is not an easy task, nor is it one that can be done and truly worked in you by your own might. You must leave behind your fleshly desires that have ruled over you for most of your life. Pride must go. You must be willing to be offended without taking offense. You must accept rejection and realize that, sometimes, you will be humiliated. Even though it hurts deeply, remember that the One who loved you and saved you has never and will never reject you. He went through all that first for you so that, by abiding in Him, you also will overcome. He bore everything for us at the Cross. There is nothing that will ever separate us from His love:

Can anything ever separate us from Christ's love? Does it mean he no longer loves us if we have trouble or calamity, or are persecuted, or hungry, or destitute, or in danger, or threatened with death? . . . No, despite all these things, overwhelming victory is ours through Christ, who loved us. And I am convinced that nothing can ever separate us from God's love. Neither death nor life, neither angels nor demons, neither our fears for today nor our worries about tomorrow – not even the powers of hell can separate us from God's love. No power in the sky above or in the earth below – indeed, nothing in all creation will ever be able to

separate us from the love of God that is
revealed in Christ Jesus our Lord.
– Romans 8:35,37-39 (NLT)

Because I knew the One in whom I had believed,
I decided to walk in front of my husband's eyes,
projecting Christ's love with my actions, to let him know
that what I was living was real. I wanted him to see that
the Lord had truly touched my life, and that I had truly
repented and had been forgiven. I wanted to show him
by my actions that I loved him and forgave him for the
many sorrows and rejections, in the same manner that
the Lord forgave and loved me.

*For the sake of your marriage, you must choose
to carry your cross and follow Him. What is your cross?
My cross was to go through the great storm in order to
win my husband and my family back, for myself and –
most of all – for Christ.*

Again I ask, what is your cross?

CHAPTER VIII
Resting in GOD'S Arms

Persevering through such a time was not easy. There were good days, and there were bad days. On the bad days, my husband would remind me constantly of my failure. I could understand this, because I had experienced the same anger when he was unfaithful to me. As you may remember, the sin I despised most in my husband was the one I ended up falling into myself. I knew his pain. This knowledge allowed me to extend grace when he was in that frame of mind; it never made it easier, but it helped me choose not to take offense. I understood the Word of God: **when the Lord sets you free, you are free indeed (John 8:36)**. I held on to those words, knowing that I was forgiven, even when my husband's anger drove him to make me relive my shame.

This season of my life caused me to think deeply on the question Jesus asks in **Matthew 5**: what reward are you going to get, loving those who love you? The truth is, the reward comes when you love those who hate you or oppose you – your enemies. **"'But I say to you, Love your enemies and pray for those who persecute you, so that you may be sons of your Father who is in heaven. For he makes his sun rise on the evil and on the good, and sends rain on the just and on the unjust. For if you love those who love you, what reward do you have?'" – Matthew 5:44-46a (ESV)**

On the good days, he treated me well and we engaged in normal family life – dining together, even talking and laughing together. On those days, it seemed like the redemption I had been eagerly praying and waiting for had come, but it never lasted. We would always fall back into the same pattern of anger, torment, and disillusionment.

Still, regardless of the cycle of good and bad days, I focused on what I wanted and didn't allow the changes in my daily circumstances to affect my vision. That is why it is so important to know Scripture promises that can help you live and act according to each day's situation. Whether your day is good or bad, if you walk accordingly, His promises will guard and protect you. That way, when the bad days come and when they end, you will stand firm.

Therefore take up the whole armor of God, that you may be able to withstand in the evil day, and having done all, to stand firm. Stand therefore, having fastened on the belt of truth, and having put on the breastplate of righteousness, and, as shoes for your feet, having put on the readiness given by the gospel of peace. In all circumstances take up the shield of faith, with which you can extinguish all the flaming darts of the evil one; and take the helmet of salvation, and the sword of the Spirit, which is the word of God, praying at all times in the Spirit, with all prayer and supplication.
– Ephesians 6:13-18a (ESV)

I had a great understanding at that point that the Lord was, and is, and always will be faithful to His Word, so I acted on His Word while waiting for His promises to come true in my life. I chose to love my husband, even though he was too angry to love me.

Several months passed after my return to Panama. The family was, in a literal sense, back together. During this time, a member of my church prophesied to me that I was going to get pregnant. It was said to me that I was going to have a girl, and that she was going to be a blessing to my husband and to the family. A short time after, I conceived. The promise of a daughter was confirmed through a vision I had in which my daughter was presented to me. This vision gave me certainty that our daughter was coming and that she was going to be, indeed, a blessing to the family.

The day of my delivery came. The Lord was faithful, and I did give birth to a girl. This stirred up my faith that, soon enough, maybe things would turn around for my family – that our time of blessing had come. We named her Johana Delaia, which means "gift of God" and "the Lord has blessed". She definitely was a beautiful gift, and she brought joy to my husband's heart.

Three months after I had Johana, I found out I was with child again. Once more, the Lord showed me in a vision that it was going to be a girl. Our fifth child was born nine months later. We named her Shaila, which means "welcome". We decided to give her this name because it was difficult in the beginning for us to accept another pregnancy so quickly; but, His will is better than ours, so we welcomed her and were at peace. We were happy with our boys, but I believe the Lord gave us our girls to work something beautiful in my husband's heart. A visible change began to occur in him, and I quite enjoyed what I was witnessing.

Throughout these events, I kept my peace by praying and seeking His guidance, even though it was sometimes very hard to ride those terrible and strong winds brought on by the storm. When you know the One in whom you believe, you find refuge in His arms and in His presence. The Lord always reminded me that if I was in Christ, I was a new creature. My past was gone, and He had for me a new beginning **(2 Cor 5:17)**. This is true for anyone who believes in Christ as their Savior. Anyone who belongs to Christ has become a new person; the old has passed away.

CHAPTER IX
The Answer to Years of Prayer

I thank the Lord for the church family that God gave me at that time. They knew how to show the love of Christ in life-changing ways. They loved my husband exactly as he was without expecting anything from him. At this point in his life, my husband was struggling with alcohol abuse. It was not caused by our marital strain, but was already present when we first married. I dealt with it along with everything else.

The church family was so accepting of him, exactly as he was, that he was always invited whenever the church was having family picnics or events. They knew of his condition. They knew that, if my husband showed up, he would bring his beers. The pastor, a very gracious man, never permitted anyone to tell him he was not allowed to. This really touched me because I knew how strongly the church discouraged alcohol consumption within its membership. But their love for us showed when, instead of condemning my husband's drinking habits at their events, they welcomed him with open arms. They even allowed my husband to put his beer in the church coolers along with their waters and other beverages! This may not seem like a big deal, but it was for my husband.

Before I continue, I would like to add here that my belief isn't that Christians should not drink alcohol, nor is it that they should. It is my belief that one should exercise self-control in everything. I believe that alcohol should not have control over a person; the person should maintain control over their consumption. If having control is too difficult, then I pray that person would come to the conclusion to abstain.

I believe that the love this church family displayed towards my husband played a big role in helping him to understand and receive the love of Christ. After all, Christ doesn't wait for us to have it all together, but calls us and accepts as we are, even in our darkest and most broken times. **Romans 5:8 (NLT) "But God showed his great love for us by sending Christ to die for us while we were still sinners."**

Three years after my return to Panama, my church hosted an evangelist from New York, a former professional boxer. It is a funny thing how God uses our interests to draw us in. My husband used to be a boxer and still loves the sport to this day. This was the perfect event for him. I invited my husband, he accepted my invitation, and we attended a church service together for the first time. The evangelist gave his testimony and described how the Lord had forgiven and delivered him. My husband was very attentive. When it came time for the evangelist to close, he made an invitation to those who wanted to accept the Lord as their Savior. My husband was the only one to raise his hand.

That day, he accepted Jesus Christ as his personal Savior.

Praise God!

It is amazing how attentive and intentional God is for each lost soul. It was as if this event was specifically for my husband. Everyone rejoiced, both inwardly and outwardly. My eldest son could not sit still because of the excitement in his heart over his father's decision to accept God's love. At that moment, the memories of all the times I had tried to encourage Steven came rushing through my mind like a flood: all the times I told him that, one day, his father would come to know the Lord – that things in our family would change – that, one day, he would see his father walking into church with a Bible in his hand.

As if this miracle were not enough reason for praise, my husband was delivered from alcohol abuse immediately following his conversion. It was a joyful moment. My family was facing a new road, walking together in the Lord.

For three years, I prayed, fasted, and waited for the Lord to touch my husband – and, finally, the time had come. My Savior was faithful to His promise. All I could and still do say is that God is more than able. *For Him, nothing is impossible.*

CHAPTER X
Rejection

Shortly after my husband's conversion, we were sent back to the U.S. We didn't realize it immediately, but this was the start of a new journey for us. Our Christian walk together was going to be one of healing, but our new location held unexpected difficulties.

We found a church home in NC, and soon, we shared our story with them. We thought it was a witness to the great things God can do. Unfortunately, the unconditional love we had experienced at our previous church was not what we encountered at this one. Some did not receive our story well, and we were judged harshly – both of us. My husband was often ridiculed as a weak man because of his willingness to continue in our marriage. As for me, well, I was seen and made to feel without a shadow of a doubt as the main character in Nathaniel Hawthorne's novel *The Scarlet Letter*.

In this novel, Hester Prynne is caught in the act of adultery and made to wear a crimson-colored letter "A" on her chest: a symbol of her sin and shame, for all to know what she had done. Like me, she faced harsh judgment and cruel treatment because of her sin. I could only imagine the weight of the burden she was forced to carry, and often empathized with Hester's situation. Moreover, I believed I knew what the woman caught in adultery and brought to Jesus **(John 8:3-11)** was feeling in that moment. I often found myself facing similar judgment and ridicule, from those in the church as well as from the world.

You see, in the eyes of many, a cheater will always be a cheater. This is a concept developed by the world, but in the church body – where repentance, forgiveness, redemption, and the cleansing of one's sin are taught – you can still find some believers embracing this worldly notion. Some, when fellow believers have fallen, continue to hold them under the weight of their past sin, not allowing them to experience the freedom given to them by our merciful Savior. We tend to forget that when there is true repentance, and when we receive the sacrifice of Jesus on the cross, His precious blood is mighty to save and cleanse us from all our sins.

But, we have hope, even in the midst of the rejection. The crimson color of Hester's letter of shame also points to Christ's cleansing power and redemption for us all, the crimson stain that is referred to in **Isaiah 1:18 (NIV): "'Come now, let us *settle the matter,'*** (emphasis mine) **says the Lord. 'Though your sins are like scarlet, they shall be as white as snow; though they are red as crimson, they shall be like wool.'"**

Whether the sin is great or small, all sin is the same in the eyes of God. We are all in need of repentance and salvation. We have come to His feet, surrendering it all, and God has forgiven us. So, let us leave all judgment aside and not force the "adulterous woman", after she has repented, to wear the scarlet letter for the rest of her life. God has so graciously forgiven the repentant adulterer, and the "scarlet letter" no longer exists for those who have truly repented.

I know that my husband, at times, had to feel horribly humiliated by the judgment of other men for the sin I had committed – the sin he forgave. It was in these moments that my husband finally began to understand my suffering with rejection. He knew he had experienced God's cleansing and salvation, yet the harsh judgment of others kept him from enjoying his freedom. This new understanding led him to become, after the Holy Spirit, my greatest comforter. I can now say that he is the one who always helps me carry my deepest pain. This was just one way our loving God brought good out of the evil surrounding us.

45

I think the most difficult part of this story is that we received this treatment from our brothers and sisters in Christ. Hear me, dear ones: ***extending forgiveness is the key for you to endure such times!*** When you know the Word of God and understand what He has done for you, you can detach rapidly from the condemnation of man. If you repent from your sin and find yourself in a similarly judgmental situation, remember that His blood has cleansed you. Just as the Word of God states, you are a new creature in Christ once you repent and are born again:

> **So we have stopped evaluating others from a human point of view. At one time we thought of Christ merely from a human point of view. How differently we know Him now! This means that anyone who belongs to Christ has become a new person. The old life is gone; a new life has begun!**
> **– 2 Corinthians 5:16-17 (NLT)**

These are promises that you will have to hold on to in order to maintain strength and faith. Judgment is never easy to endure, but it does grow more tolerable as time goes on and as we constantly seek the Lord, holding on to His Word. Always remember this: ***never*** *take your eyes from the Lord.* Seek a close relationship and fellowship with Him every day, believing that all His promises are true. **Hebrews 12:2 (NLT) "We do this by keeping our eyes on Jesus, the champion who initiates and perfects our faith. Because of the joy awaiting Him, He endured the cross, disregarding its shame."**

And so can you!

Needless to say, we eventually left this church and found a new home for our family that truly practiced the word of God. I began to see a change in my husband: from pride to humility, from anger to gentleness, from a hard heart to a heart constantly seeking God. The beauty of God's work in my husband's life continued to unfold before my eyes day after day, and the power of His might was evident in my life as well.

CHAPTER XI
Refuge

Even after his conversion and his acceptance of our situation, my husband struggled back and forth with unforgiveness. His battle with this stronghold lasted for around sixteen years. I could see his willingness to change and totally extend the forgiveness that I craved, but his old self continued to fight. At moments, it looked like he had it all "together"; but, when least expected, his manly pride came back like a raging bull. When he behaved this way, my faith in what I was waiting for was truly tested.

It is a painful thing to be reminded of your past when you no longer live there. I can relate it to walking into an immaculate room that evokes feelings of comfort and peace. Then, someone comes and intentionally dirties this clean and peaceful place. The room becomes so dirty that you no longer can enjoy it, but instead feel a deep displeasure and discomfort. Once the discomfort finally passes, you remember that you already have all the necessary tools to restore your once immaculate room to its former condition. (What I am referring to here as "tools" are the great and powerful promises given to us by God through His son Jesus Christ.) So, you move forward, using these tools to restore the room, and finding your feelings of comfort and peace restored also.

I lived that allegory on numerous occasions when I felt accused and untrustworthy. Sixteen years passed while we were on this journey, and though it was often more challenging than we would have liked, we were able to endure – and, eventually, overcome! – only by the faith that God put in our hearts. We overcame by submitting ourselves to the Lord and to what He was expecting from us. Believe me when I say that you really have to die to your own selfish desires in order to be able to practice what the Lord has told you to do.

What our children witnessed along the way was by no means easy for them, as our testimony and struggles were never hidden. We have spoken to each of our children and have sought their forgiveness for every wrong action that they witnessed during our trial and restoration. We know that what we went through caused harm to them. I can honestly and freely say that some of our children still find it difficult to trust.

Whenever I have the chance to teach and guide them in this area, I do. It is safe to say that this struggle of theirs can only be dealt with by the Lord Himself. I continue to pray for total healing for them. I am confident that the Lord will deliver them from all damage done by the past.

If you are feeling regret and guilt because of the pain that your actions have caused your children, I strongly suggest you to *"trust in the Lord and in the power of His might".* Release your children through prayer to God's guidance and loving care: "*He will not leave or forsake them".* The Lord will protect not only them, but also the family as a whole! **Trust Him!** As the Lord was my refuge in my desperate situation, He will be yours too.

> **God is our refuge and strength, an ever-present help in trouble. Therefore, we will not fear, though the earth give way and the mountains fall into the heart of the sea, though its waters roar and foam and the mountains quake with their surging. . . . The Lord Almighty is with us; the God of Jacob is our fortress."**
>
> **– Psalm 46:1-3,7 (NIV)**

I am thankful that the Lord was true to His promise: He was and is our refuge.

CHAPTER XII
Surprising Results

From the moment I accepted Christ into my life, I had and still have a burden to pray and intercede for the adulterous woman. I have had opportunities to minister to other women who have fallen just as I have, and I have been able to encourage them, sharing in prayer and in faith. Everyone has a different story, and the results of repentance are sometimes surprising. Two particular friends come to mind whose stories show just how varied our paths can be.

A Story of Redemption

I will not disclose the name of this friend, but will use the name Maria.

We met overseas on my family's last tour to Germany. Over the years, we developed a beautiful friendship. I will never forget that day: Nov 17, 1991. She called with a simple request for me to cut her hair. I was a hairdresser at that time. I informed her that it was my birthday, but that I really didn't mind and that she should come over. While I was cutting her hair, we engaged in fairly insignificant small talk, or so I thought. She told me about her recent travels to Puerto Rico and how she learned while there that her brother had become a Christian. She was not a believer and seemed indifferent to the idea of Christianity.

I finished her hair, and when she went to pay me, she found that her wallet was missing. She left, promising to return to pay me for my work. I thought nothing of it and told her not to worry. I even told her I would pray for an angel to guard the wallet and bring it to her. She searched her home but still could not locate her wallet. When she left her house to try and retrace her steps, her neighbor called her over. The neighbor told Maria that a tall white man had stopped by her house, and that since she hadn't been home at the time, he had stopped by the neighbor's home to drop off Maria's wallet. He explained that he knew where to go because of the information on her driver's license and her military ID, and he wanted to be sure that the wallet was safely returned to her.

When the neighbor informed Maria of all that had happened, she immediately remembered my prayer. She believed in her heart that this was the angel I had prayed for. God used this to stir up faith in her heart, along with the desire to be saved, just like her brother. Upon returning to my house, she opened up and discussed things with me that I was not aware of, as if to relieve herself of long-held secrets. Her heart was vulnerable, soft, and open. During this time, she told me about an affair that she had engaged in. She was sorrowful about it and wanted to be forgiven and saved. We prayed together, and she asked the Lord into her life. That day, she was born again.

The time came for her to confess to her husband what she had done, and she trusted in the fact that the Lord has the power to redeem. She and her husband went through a long journey of forgiveness, redemption and restoration, but God's grace is greater than our weakness, and their marriage withstood the storm. They pressed on together in forgiveness and grace. In fact, both Maria and her husband are in ministry, pastoring a Hispanic congregation in Phoenix, Arizona. Ever since that day in November, 1991, she has walked with Christ by her side.

A Story of Unforgiveness

Unfortunately, not all stories work out like Maria's. I can recall the story of another friend who fell into the same temptation of adultery. She was a dear friend in Christ and fell into this sin while being a believer. She even left her husband to live with the other man. But, the Holy Spirit convicted her, and she came to understand the gravity of her mistake in the light of the Word of God. She knew that she needed to repent and seek forgiveness, from the Lord and from her husband.

The time came, and she did what she knew she needed to do. Her heart was broken, and she was fully repentant. She asked for her husband's forgiveness, but he refused. Soon after her true repentance, he requested a divorce. Divorce was not what she wanted; but, understanding her wrongdoing and realizing the hurt she had caused, she accepted with sorrow his response to the situation. She suffered greatly, but still went on with her life. Even today, she still has to face the fact of his unforgiveness.

I have kept in contact with this friend, and I have witnessed the power of God working healing in her life, even amidst the suffering. Though her journey has been a difficult one, today she is still a child of God that continues to seek Him and His mercies. I thank God for each opportunity to impart my love and to reassure her, time and again, that the Father still has his loving arms around her. Up to this day, every time my husband and I go to Puerto Rico, we pay her a visit. I love her warrior heart, and the way she has found healing and refuge in her Savior's arms. Her healing is obvious through her faithful commitment to the Lord!

Unfortunately, we must accept that unforgiveness or divorce will sometimes happen. We really don't want to let go of what we love, but we also have to understand that our sin, no matter how repentant we are, will have consequences. In such a case, the offended party has the right to divorce if he or she desires. Still, I would counsel them to reflect prayerfully on these words of Jesus:

> **And Pharisees came up to him and tested him by asking, "Is it lawful to divorce one's wife for any cause?" He answered, "Have you not read that he who created them from the beginning made them male and female, and said, 'Therefore a man shall leave his father and his mother and hold fast to his wife, and the two shall become one flesh'? So they are no longer two but one flesh. What therefore God has joined together, let not man separate." They said to him, "Why then did Moses command one to give a certificate of divorce and to send her away?" He said**

to them, "Because of your hardness of heart Moses allowed you to divorce your wives, but from the beginning it was not so. And I say to you: whoever divorces his wife, except for sexual immorality, and marries another, commits adultery."
– Matthew 19:3-9 (ESV)

But, even if divorce occurs, never should we as believers be unforgiving – not as children of God. As the Word says in **Matthew 18:21-22 (ESV): "Then Peter came up and said to him, 'Lord, how often will my brother sin against me, and I forgive him? As many as seven times?' Jesus said to him, 'I do not say to you seven times, but seventy-seven times.'"** Jesus's whole point here is that we are supposed to go well beyond what we believe we should or can do when it comes to forgiveness. In reality, the answer is always to forgive. But, because of pride or a hardened heart, some will find this difficult and will not extend forgiveness to the one who offended or sinned against them. This in itself is a sin, and it inflicts pain on both sides.

If you have been offended by this sin in your spouse, remember that they are your brother or sister as well! The choice is yours to walk away from the marriage, but you do not have a choice about forgiving the one who has hurt you. If you find yourself struggling with unforgiveness because of this offense, also remember these words from **Matthew 6:14 (NIV) "'For if you forgive other people when they sin against you, your heavenly Father will also forgive you.'"**

I will always thank God for the way He worked in my husband's heart, allowing him finally to forgive and allowing us to remain one. May God grant you also the power to forgive.

CHAPTER XIII
Our Result

Our 30th wedding anniversary was approaching, and after much discussion, my husband and I decided to celebrate by bringing our marriage – our covenant – before God. I believe in the value of presenting your union to the Lord for His blessings. This was something we had never done previously. The planning for our "wedding" began, and the pastor of our home church – the church we still attend today – agreed to marry us.

The day of our wedding came: June 26, 1999. It was a day to remember. Our children were the bridal party: our eldest son, Steven, walked me down the aisle; Omar and Kristian were my husband's best men; Johana and Shaila were my bridesmaids. We were able to share our testimony with our guests and tell them why we were taking such steps before God. It was a surreal moment: beautiful in every way, and full of joy and tears for both Juan and me. We couldn't believe we were celebrating such an event!

After that moment, our marriage changed drastically. There were still struggles, but we knew that we were working with God to build a good marriage – one with loyalty, forgiveness, grace, perseverance, and trust. Yes, I wrote it right: TRUST. Only by God's power have we been able to trust one another again. After our wedding day, my husband forgave me, once and for all. Remember a few chapters ago? It was a long, hard, sixteen-year journey; but, when you trust God, it is amazing to see what He can do with your life – even with your seemingly overwhelming problems. Since that day of receiving God's blessing on our covenant, our marriage has been on the path of redemption, and we have been blessed to see our union and ministry bear such beautiful fruit.

My husband has had the opportunity to volunteer and serve in the Hispanic Service at our home church: "Manna Servicio en Español". He began by serving wherever he was needed, and then took over leadership by the request of the senior pastor. His passion and loyalty to the Hispanic community and to this church have grown and have also borne fruit. On September 15, 2016, my husband was ordained as a pastor.

To me, this is the most beautiful gift that the Lord has given to me. I am a witness to the miracle that took place in my husband's life. I now have a husband who has learned to love me unconditionally. He pampers me and treats me like a "fragile vessel". He has become a wise and gentle-spirited man who leads his home and ministry in a manner that edifies others and exemplifies Christ in his life. God has truly granted me the desires of my heart. My husband has earned back my deepest admiration and respect, and has also won my heart again.

As for me, the Lord has given me the gift of teaching His Word, and also the gift of encouraging fellow believers in distress. I truly love what the Lord has done: miraculously, through Jesus – my beloved Savior – my Father in heaven has given me breakthrough in what was once a great burden to bear. Through His Holy Spirit, God gave me the power to overcome, and He still carries me in His loving arms. I am grateful to Him for traveling this journey with us, and for imparting counsel, guidance and wisdom along the way. Most of all, I am grateful that he has always taught us how to keep living in His unconditional love, grace, trust, and forgiveness.

The burden remains heavy on my heart for the women who know my story because it is their own – the women who have fallen or will fall into the pit of adultery. I still intercede for them. If this is you, dear reader, know that I am praying for you – and I will always, until the day He calls me home.

CHAPTER XIV
What to Do Now

I want to bring you back to the scripture that first gave me confidence that God is a forgiving God – the Scripture in which my story is based.

Early in the morning he came again to the temple. All the people came to him, and he sat down and taught them. The scribes and the Pharisees brought a woman who had been caught in adultery, and placing her in the midst they said to him, "Teacher, this woman has been caught in the act of adultery. Now in the Law, Moses commanded us to stone such women. So what do you say?" This they said to test him, that they might have some charge to bring

against him. Jesus bent down and wrote with his finger on the ground. And as they continued to ask him, he stood up and said to them, "Let him who is without sin among you be the first to throw a stone at her." And once more he bent down and wrote on the ground. But when they heard it, they went away one by one, beginning with the older ones, and Jesus was left alone with the woman standing before him. Jesus stood up and said to her, "Woman, where are they? Has no one condemned you?" She said, "No one, Lord." And Jesus said, *"Neither do I condemn you; go, and from now on sin no more."* (emphasis mine)

– John 8: 2-11(ESV)

As I still have your attention, I want to take this opportunity to inquire: where are you in your life? Have you been impacted by the devastating consequences of adultery? Whether the one trapped in this sin's path of destruction is you or your spouse, do you believe that the Lord can set you both free and restore your marriage? If the answer to these questions is yes, please allow me to give you a few steps to follow. Afterwards, we will pray together so you can experience His forgiving grace by receiving our Lord as your loving, personal Savior.

1. If you have found yourself trapped in adultery, it is imperative that you truly repent.

2. You have to believe in your heart that the merciful God in heaven will forgive you!

3. You have to give your life to God, believe in your heart that Jesus Christ died for you on Calvary's cross to forgive you of your sins, and be cleansed by His blood.

4. If the one who has fallen is your spouse, and he/she has sought your forgiveness, ask the Lord to grant you His forgiving power. By His grace, forgive your spouse.

5. If you and your spouse are not followers of Christ, give your lives to the One – Jesus – who can redeem and restore your lives and your marriage.

6. Commit yourselves to the healing process by leaving the past behind and starting brand-new. The healing process is one of practicing forgiveness and trust daily. There will be suffering involved, so seek Him in prayer every day and ask Him for the strength to

endure. You can hold on to these promises in His Word:

- "Therefore, if anyone is in Christ, he is a new creation. The old has passed away; behold, the new has come." – 2 Corinthians 5:17 (ESV)

- "I sought the Lord, and He answered me and delivered me from all my fears." – Psalm 34:4 (ESV)

- "I called out to the Lord, out of my distress, and He answered me." – Jonah 2:2 (ESV)

- "'I have said these things to you, that in me you may have peace. In the world you will have tribulation. But take heart; I have overcome the world.'"
  – John 16:33 (ESV)

Jesus spoke these words to His disciples, and also to you!

7. Seek His wisdom to act according to His will for you and your family.

8. Confess your sin – and remember the possibility of getting unexpected results. (See the story of unforgiveness in Chapter XII.) No matter what happens, lift your head high and know that the Father in heaven has forgiven you!

Let us pray:

Father in heaven, I come to you in repentance for what I have done. Forgive me and wash me clean, as white as snow, with Your blood that was shed when You were crucified for me. Forgive me. Come into my life and make it right. I receive you today as my Lord and Savior. I give you my life, and I ask that you would restore my life and my marriage. I want to believe that you can restore all things, so I am claiming today that I believe. I give You thanks. In Jesus's name I pray. Amen.

You are now a child of the Most High King!

Now, if you are a child of God, pray, confess, repent, and ask for forgiveness.

Then, "go and sin no more".

The road you now embark on will not always be an easy one, but the Lord will walk with you every step of the way. It is His promise.

Be strong and courageous,

do not be afraid or tremble at them,

for the LORD your God is the one who goes with you.

He will not fail you or forsake you.

Deuteronomy 31:6 (NASB)

93502582R00045

Made in the USA
Columbia, SC
14 April 2018